MW01282085

·PALEO·
SLOW
COOKER

40 DELICIOUS GLUTEN FREE PALEO SLOW COOKER RECIPES TO KICK-START WEIGHT LOSS

Disclaimer

The information in this book is not to be used as medical advice. The recipes should be used in combination with guidance from your physician. Please consult your physician before beginning any diet. It is especially important for those with diabetes, and those on medications to consult with their physician before making changes to their diet.

Disclaimer and Terms of Use: Effort has been made to ensure that the information in this book is accurate and complete, however, the author and the publisher do not warrant the accuracy of the information, text and graphics contained within the book due to the rapidly changing nature of science, research, known and unknown facts and internet. The Author and the publisher do not hold any responsibility for errors, omissions or contrary interpretation of the subject matter herein. This book is presented solely for motivational and informational purposes only.

Introduction

The Paleolithic lifestyle outlined in this recipe book is truly life-altering. Your days of counting carbohydrates, counting calories, and counting fat can finally come to an end as you return to what your body yearns to eat: the very things your ancestors ate some two thousand years ago. Our digestive system hasn't altered at all in that time, and because of this, your body cannot digest the crazy processed things you can find so easily at the grocery store. It simply hasn't evolved to eat donuts: that's why, in a nutshell, the perpetual obesity problem persists. Our bodies are simply ill equipped to handle everything we throw in them.

"The Paleo Slow Cooker Cookbook" brings you forty recipes that yield these essential nutrients from two thousand years ago. It offers beef, pork, chicken, lamb, and vegetable based meals that allow you to lose weight and reduce interior bodily problems, such as uncomfortable bloating caused by irritants in carbohydrates. Each recipe promotes healthy fats from olive oils, coconut oils, and grass-fed meat.

Proponents of the Paleolithic diet state that they have greater energy levels, healthy-looking hair, muscle growth that led to greater weight loss, an increased level of insulin sensitivity, a decrease in depression and anxiety feelings, and several other benefits. Your body begins working precisely as it's supposed to when you give it the food it needs.

The slow cooker is the perfect utensil to elevate your Paleolithic diet plan, as well, because the meat you'll be preparing really enriches in flavor the longer it cooks. Set aside the baby back ribs in the slow cooker for some eight hours, and you'll find them falling off the bone and ready for succulent eating when you return. All the flavors begin to assimilate together, work with each other, to form a sort of medley. Oregano, basil, garlic, sweet potatoes—the flavor list is endless—orchestrate something very essential for your end-of-the workday routine. You'll find that while you were out living your very crazy life, your slow cooker was at home creating a masterpiece for you: something you could never have created yourself in your ramen-noodle-microwave-schedule lifestyle.

Begin to live well with these forty recipes. Create breakfast recipes for guests, find fruit and cocao-based dessert recipes for your next celebration, or soups and stews for your next sick day. Alternately, create the next game-day ribs, the next family gathering curry—or one of the many other options outlined in this recipe book. You can live an elevated lifestyle with the assistance of the Paleolithic diet and its marriage to the slow cooker. Create warmth and hearty happiness in your household. Don't wait to fuel yourself with flavor and nutrition!

Table of Contents

Be Our Guest Breakfast Meatloaf

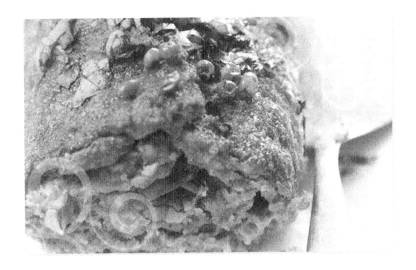

Prep Time: 10 minutes
Cook Time: 4 hours
Recipe Makes: 8 Servings
Nutritional Breakdown per Serving: 210 calories, 3 grams net carbohydrates, 19 grams fat, 22 grams protein

Ingredients:
1 ¾ pounds ground pork
1 tbsp. coconut oil
2 diced onions
½ cup almond flour
2 eggs

1 tbsp. garlic powder

3 tsp. fennel seeds

2 tsp. red pepper flakes

1 tsp. pepper

1 tsp. paprika

2 tbsp. maple syrup

Directions:

Begin by softening the onions in the coconut oil for about five minutes. Remove the onions from the heat and set them to the side. Next, bring together all of the other ingredients into a large bowl. Stir well in order to assimilate them. Toss in the onions and begin to fold and manipulate the meatloaf until you've created a loaf-like mixture. Pick up this "loaf" and place it in the center of the slow cooker.

Place the lid on the slow cooker and cook for a full three hours on HIGH.

Sweet Potato Pork Breakfast Casserole

Prep Time: 10 minutes
Cook Time: 8 hours
Recipe makes: 6 Servings
Nutritional Breakdown per Serving: 210 calories, 3 grams net carbohydrates, 18 grams fat, 24 grams protein

Ingredients:
8 eggs
1 shredded sweet potato
¾ pound diced pork sausage
2 tsp. basil
1 diced onion
1 tbsp. garlic powder
1 diced green pepper

Directions:
Begin by shredding the sweet potato in a food processor. Add the eggs to the slow cooker, first, and whisk them well with a fork. Next, add the spices and the prepared vegetables: basil, onion, sweet potato, garlic powder, and the green pepper. Stir the ingredients well, and finally add the pork sausage. Afterwards, place the lid on the slow cooker and cook for eight hours on LOW. Enjoy!

Sausage and Butternut Squash Breakfast Casserole

Prep Time: 10 minutes
Cook time: 10 hours
Recipe Makes 8 Servings
Nutritional Breakdown per Serving: 195 calories, 4 grams net carbohydrates, 16 grams fat, 14 grams protein

Ingredients:
¾ pound sausage
2 diced onions
12 eggs
1 ½ butternut squash
1 cup coconut milk

Directions:
Begin by browning the sausage in a skillet with a bit of olive oil. Dice up the onion and add the onion to the sausage. When the onion begins to look clear, pour the skillet's contents into the slow cooker.

To the side, mix together the coconut milk and the eggs.

Prepare the butternut squash be peeling it, de-seeding it, and slicing it up. Place the squash overtop the sausage and pour in the egg and coconut milk mixture. Stir well and cook the casserole on LOW for ten hours. Enjoy.

BEEF BASED
SLOW
COOKER
RECIPES

Spiced-Up Giardiniera and Italian Beef

Prep Time: 2 days
Cook Time: 8 hours
Recipe Makes 10 Servings
Nutritional Breakdown per Serving: 250 calories, 3 grams net carbohydrates, 27 grams fat, 20 grams protein

Giardiniera Ingredients:
2 cups diced carrots
2 cups chopped cauliflower
1 diced red pepper
3 sliced Serrano peppers

1 tsp. oregano

3 minced garlic cloves

½ cup apple cider vinegar

1 cup olive oil

1 tsp. thyme

Italian Beef Ingredients:

½ cup water

3 pounds beef pot roast

5 minced garlic cloves

1 quartered onion

1 tsp. thyme

1 ½ tsp. oregano

Directions:

Begin two days before you plan to create your Italian Beef recipe. You must bring together all of the chopped vegetables from the Giardiniera list in a bowl. Cover the bowl and allow it to refrigerate for a full twelve hours. Afterwards, mix together the vinegar, oil, thyme, and oregano. Pour this mixture overtop the prepared vegetables and stir well. Allow the vegetables to marinate for an additional twenty-four hours.

Eight hours before your marinade is completed, you can begin your Italian beef. Bring all of the beef ingredients into the slow cooker and allow all the liquid and herbs to coat the beef. Cook the slow cooker on LOW for eight hours. When you're ready, serve the prepared marinade with the Italian beef. Enjoy.

Coffee and Jazzed-Up Beef Roast

Prep Time: 20 minutes
Cook Time: 6 hours
Recipe Makes 8 Servings
Nutritional Breakdown per Serving: 210 calories, 4 grams net carbohydrates, 15 grams fat, 15 grams protein

Coffee Rub Ingredients:

3 tbsp. ground coffee

1 tbsp. pepper

3 tbsp. paprika

1 tsp. Aleppo pepper

1 tsp. chili powder

1 tsp. ginger

1 tbsp. cocoa powder

Roast Ingredients:

1 ¾ pounds beef roast

1 cup beef broth

1 ½ cups pre-brewed coffee

3 chopped figs

3 chopped dates

1 diced onion

4 tbsp. balsamic vinegar

Directions:

Begin by bringing together the various spices and mixing them in a little bowl. Next, rub this mixture into the beef with a napkin or with your hand. Really dig into it, allowing the mixture to touch every surface.

To the side, combine the broth, coffee, dates, fibs, onion, and the vinegar in a food processor or blender. Create its liquid equivalent. Next, pour this created liquid into the slow cooker and place the beef on top. Cook on LOW for six hours. Afterwards, remove the beef and shred it with forks. Salt and pepper the result, and enjoy.

St. Patrick's Paleo Corned Beef and Cabbage

Prep Time: 20 minutes
Cook Time: 9 hours
Recipe Makes 8 Servings
Nutritional Breakdown per Serving: 240 calories, 2 grams net carbohydrates, 19 grams fat, 27 grams protein

Ingredients:
8 chopped carrots
1 wedged cabbage
3 diced onions
2 ½ pounds corned beef brisket
1 corned beef seasoning pack (found at local grocery store)
2 ½ cups water

Directions:
Prepare the vegetables and toss them in the slow cooker. Afterwards, place the beef in the slow cooker and sprinkle over the corned beef seasoning pack, making sure to get the mixture into every ridge of the meat.

Add the water to the slow cooker and cook on LOW for nine hours. Afterwards, serve the corned beef with the cooking juices from the slow cooker overtop. Enjoy!

Steamy Beef Stroganoff

Prep Time: 15 minutes
Cook Time: 8 hours
Recipe Makes 4 Servings
Nutritional Breakdown per Serving: 280 calories, 4 grams net carbohydrates, 24 grams fat, 27 grams protein

Ingredients:

1 pound sliced sirloin steak

2 diced onions

6 tbsp. coconut oil

1 ½ cups beef stock

8 ounces sliced mushrooms

3 minced garlic cloves

1 cup coconut milk

¼ cup white wine

salt and pepper to taste

Directions:

Begin by browning the sirloin steak in a bit of olive or coconut oil in a skillet. This should take about five minutes. Afterwards, place the meat in the slow cooker.

To the side, prepare the onions, mushrooms and the garlic cloves. Place this layer of vegetables over the sirloin. Pour in the remaining ingredients: coconut oil, coconut milk, white wine, and the salt and pepper. Stir well, and place the lid on the slow cooker. Cook on LOW for eight hours. Serve warm.

PORK BASED SLOW COOKER RECIPES

Cinco-Spiced Crockpot Pork Ribs

Prep Time: 10 minutes
Cook time: 10 hours
Recipe Makes 12 Servings
Nutritional Breakdown per Serving: 275 calories, 2 grams net carbohydrates per serving, 27 grams fat, 32 grams protein

Ingredients:

3 ½ pounds pork ribs

2 tsp. garlic powder

2 tsp. basil

2 tsp. cumin

2 tsp. paprika

2 tsp. red pepper flakes

1 sliced jalapeno

3 tbsp. coconut aminos

2 tbsp. rice vinegar

1 ½ tbsp. tomato paste

Directions:

Begin by slicing the ribs into smaller pieces that you can actually stand up straight in the slow cooker. Prior to actually doing this, salt them and pepper them. To the side, mix together the various other spices, and then massage the spices onto the ribs as well.

Place the sliced jalapeno at the bottom of the slow cooker, followed by the coconut aminos, the rice vinegar, and the tomato paste. Stir this concoction well. Then, stand up the ribs in the slow cooker so that they're not directly in the sauce. Place the cover on the slow cooker and cook on LOW for approximately ten hours.

Afterwards, remove the ribs from the slow cooker and keep them warm. Remove the fat from the slow cooker and bring the sauce in the interior of the slow cooker to boil. This will be your sauce for the ribs.

Also, if you want crispy ribs, you can toss your prepared ribs into the oven for ten minutes at 400 degrees Fahrenheit.

Vamos Carnitas

Prep Time: 15 minutes
Cook Time: 8 hours
Recipe Makes 8 Servings
Nutritional Breakdown per Serving: 245 calories, 3 grams net carbohydrates, 19 grams fat, 28 grams protein

Ingredients:
3 pounds pork roast
3 tsp. oregano
1 tsp. chili powder
2 tbsp. cinnamon
5 minced garlic cloves
juice from 2 oranges
juice from 2 limes
1 diced onion
3 tbsp. melted coconut oil

Directions:
Place the pork loin roast in the slow cooker and spread the chili powder and oregano all over the meat. Afterwards, place the garlic, onion, and the cinnamon on top.

Squeeze the oranges and limes on the top of the pork and allow the pork to cook on LOW for eight hours. Next, shred up the meat and melt the coconut oil on the stove. Make the carnitas crispy in the skillet for a delightful take on an old recipe.

Aloha Hawaii Pulled Pork

Pre Time: 5 minutes
Cook time: 8 hours
Recipe Makes 6 Servings
Nutritional Breakdown per Serving: 250 calories, 15 grams net carbohydrates, 22 grams fat, 26 grams protein

Ingredients:
3 ½ pounds pork shoulder
1 ½ cups cubed pineapple
3 tbsp. ginger

Directions:
Place the pork shoulder into the slow cooker and add the pineapple overtop the pork. Toss in the ginger and stir the ginger into the pineapple. Place the lid on the slow cooker and cook the pork on LOW for eight hours. Afterwards, shred the pork with two large forks and create your delicious pulled pork.

Gala Apple Midwestern Pork Tenderloin

Prep Time: 15 minutes
Cook Time: 8 hours
Recipe Makes 8 Servings
Nutritional Breakdown Per Serving: 240 calories, 15 grams net carbohydrates, 22 grams fat, 25 grams protein

Ingredients:
4 Gala apples
1 ½ pounds pork tenderloin
1 tbsp. nutmeg
2 tbsp. honey

Directions:
Begin by coring and slicing the apples and placing a layer of the apples at the very bottom of the slow cooker. Sprinkle the nutmeg over the apples. Next, place the tenderloin at the bottom of the slow cooker. Place another layer of apples over the tenderloin. Add a bit more nutmeg, if you please.

Place the lid on the slow cooker and allow the pork to cook for 8 hours on LOW. Enjoy both the pork and the apples on the side.

Honey-Dripped Chicken Wings

Prep Time: 10 minutes
Cook Time: 6 Hours
Recipe Makes 5 Servings
Nutritional Breakdown per Serving: 250 calories, 7 grams net carbohydrates, 18 grams fat, 27 grams protein

Ingredients:

30 wings
¾ cup liquid, raw honey
3 tbsp. olive oil
2 minced garlic cloves
salt and pepper to taste

Directions:

Place all the wings in the slow cooker and, to the side, mix together the olive oil, the minced garlic, the honey, and some salt and pepper. Drizzle this mixture over the wings in the slow cooker and stir well. Cook the wings on LOW for six hours.

African Dance Moroccan Chicken

Prep Time: 20 minutes
Cook Time: 6 hours
Recipe Makes 8 Servings
Nutritional Breakdown per Serving: 280 calories, 11 grams net carbohydrates, 18 grams fat, 35 grams protein

Ingredients:

14 ounces tomato sauce

1/3 cup pureed apricots

1 tsp. ginger

1 ½ tsp. cumin

juice from 1 lemon

4 minced garlic cloves

3 ½ pounds chicken breasts

½ tsp. paprika

2 diced onions

½ cup almond butter

2 cups water

3 tbsp. coconut oil

Directions:

Bring together the pureed apricot, tomato sauce, cumin, ginger, lemon juice, paprika, and salt in a small bowl. Stir. Afterwards, heat coconut oil in a skillet and allow it to melt. Place the chicken in the skillet and allow it to scald a bit. Toss in the onions, ginger, and garlic and cook for two more minutes.

Pour this mixture into the slow cooker and add almond butter and water as well. Add all of the additional spices and stir. Allow the chicken to cook for six hours on LOW.

Athena Greek-Stuffed Chicken

Prep Time: 20 minutes
Cook Time: 8 hours
Recipe Makes 6 Servings
Nutritional Breakdown Per Serving: 250 calories, 3 grams net carbohydrates, 20 gram fat, 24 grams protein

Ingredients:

6 chicken breasts
1 tbsp. olive oil
2 sliced red peppers
1 diced onion
8 ounces spinach
1 ½ tsp. oregano
juice from 1 lemon
1 ½ cups chicken stock
¾ cup white wine
2 cloves minced garlic

Directions:

Begin by preparing the chicken. Slice the chicken in its side, creating a pocket. Salt and pepper the chicken and set them to the side.

Next, add the olive oil into a skillet and cook the onions and the peppers for about three minutes. Toss in the garlic and the spinach and cook for an additional one minute. Add oregano and remove the mixture from the heat.

Stuff the prepared pepper and onion mixture into each chicken and place each chicken in the slow cooker. Pour over the stock and the wine and allow the chicken to cook for eight hours on LOW. Enjoy!

Teriyaki Ginger Chicken

Prep Time: 5 minutes
Cook Time: 8 hours
Recipe Makes 6 Servings
Nutritional Breakdown Per Serving: 250 calories, 5 grams net carbohydrates, 18 grams fat, 22 grams protein

Ingredients:

1 ½ pounds chicken thighs

¾ cup coconut amino

2 tbsp. ground ginger

1 tbsp. honey

3 minced garlic cloves

salt and pepper to taste

Directions:

Begin by bringing together the honey, ginger, coconut aminos, and the garlic cloves. Stir well. Next, place the chicken on the bottom of the slow cooker and pour the created sauce overtop.

Cook on LOW for eight hours and salt and pepper the chicken to taste. Serve warm.

Balsamic and Peach Chicken Dinner

Prep Time: 20 Minutes
Cook Time: 8 hours
Recipe Makes 10 Servings
Nutritional Breakdown Per Serving: 210 calories, 3 grams net carbohydrates, 15 grams fat, 18 grams protein

Ingredients:
3 tbsp. olive oil
2 diced onions
4 rosemary sprigs
3 pitted and sliced peaches
1/3 cup honey
10 chicken thighs
salt and pepper to taste

Directions:
Begin by heating olive oil and onions together in a skillet. When the onions have turned translucent, pour the mixture into the slow cooker. Add the rosemary sprigs, the pitted and sliced peaches, the honey, and the ten chicken thighs to the slow cooker. Salt and pepper the tops of the chicken, and attempt to coat the

chicken with the sauce beneath it by turning it a few times. Cook on LOW for eight hours and serve warm.

LAMB BASED
SLOW
COOKER
RECIPES

Spiced Lamb Roast

Prep Time: 10 minutes
Cook Time: 7 hours
Recipe Makes 8 Servings
Nutritional Breakdown Per Serving: 210 calories, 2 grams net carbohydrates, 22 grams fat, 24 grams protein

Ingredients:
2 pounds lamb roast
8 ounces diced green chilies
2 diced green peppers
14 ounces diced tomatoes
2 tsp. garlic powder
1 tsp. chili powder
1 tbsp. cumin
salt and pepper to taste

Directions:
Place the lamb meat at the bottom of the slow cooker and add in the bell peppers, tomatoes, and the green chilies. Toss in the spices and stir well. Cook the meat on LOW for seven hours and serve warm.

Coconut Craze Lemon Curry

Prep Time: 10 minutes
Cook Time: 8 hours
Recipe Makes 3 Servings
Nutritional Breakdown per Serving: 210 calories, 2 grams net carbohydrates, 19 grams fat, 22 grams protein

Ingredients:
2 tsp. melted coconut oil
½ red chili
2 pounds diced lamb
1 diced celery stalk
1 tsp. turmeric powder
1 cup coconut milk
1 tbsp. tomato paste
¾ cup water
1 diced carrot
2 minced garlic cloves
3 tsp. garam masala

Directions:
Begin by pouring the coconut oil in a skillet and browning the lamb for five minutes. Afterwards, pour the lamb into the slow cooker and surround it with the vegetables. Pour over the coconut

milk, the tomato paste, and the water, and add all the spices. Stir well. Place the lid on the slow cooker and cook for a full eight hours on LOW. Serve warm.

Rosemary Leg of Lamb

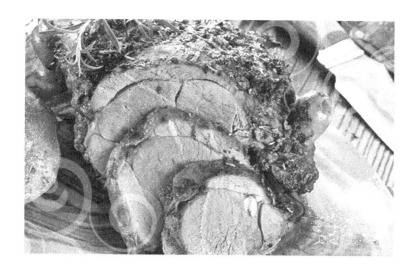

Prep Time: 5 minutes
Cook time: 8 hours
Recipe Makes 7 Servings.
Nutritional Breakdown per Serving: 240 calories, 2 grams net carbohydrates, 18 grams fat, 22 grams protein.

Ingredients:

1 leg of lamb
3 chopped rosemary sprigs
½ cup fresh mint
1 tbsp. olive oil
4 minced garlic cloves

salt

Directions:

Begin by completely drying out the leg of lamb. To the side, mix together the various herbs and the olive oil and stir well. Add this to the lamb and smear the lamb. Add salt. Place the lamb in the slow cooker and cook on LOW for eight hours. Serve warm.

Mechoui of Morocco Lamb

Prep Time: 15 minutes
Cook time: 8 hours
Recipe Makes 8 Servings
Nutritional Breakdown per Serving: 230
calories, 2 grams net carbohydrates, 22
grams fat, 23 grams protein

Ingredients:
1 lamb shoulder
4 tbsp. coconut oil
5 minced garlic cloves
1 tsp. pepper
2 tsp. salt
2 tsp. crushed saffron
2 tsp. cumin
¼ tsp. turmeric
1 ½ tbsp. olive oil

Directions:
Begin by mixing together the pre-melted coconut oil, garlic, pepper, saffron, cumin, turmeric, olive oil, and salt and pepper. Spread this mixture all over the lamb and place the lamb into the slow cooker. Cook on LOW for eight hours. Enjoy.

VEGETARIAN
SLOW
COOKER
RECIPES

Sweet Life Slow Cooker Sweet Potatoes

Prep Time: 5 minutes
Cook Time: 8 hours
Recipe Makes 10 Servings
Nutritional Breakdown Per Serving: 100 calories, 17 net carbohydrates, 0 grams fat, 2 grams protein

Ingredients:
5 sweet potatoes

Directions:
Begin by wrapping every sweet potato in a piece of foil and placing each potato in the slow cooker for eight hours on LOW. Afterwards, cut in halves and drizzle with a bit of almond butter or coconut butter to taste.

Curry-Green Bean Side Dish

Prep Time: 5 minutes.
Cook Time: 5 hours.
Recipe Makes 5 Servings
Nutritional Breakdown per Serving: 85 calories, 4 grams net carbohydrates, 8 grams fat, 3 grams protein

Ingredients:
5 cups kale
4 cups green beans
1 can vegetable stock
1 can coconut milk
1 ½ tbsp. yellow curry powder

Directions:
Pour the stock and the coconut milk into the slow cooker and stir in the curry powder. Afterwards, pour in the green beans and the kale. Stir well, and allow the beans to cook for five hours on LOW.

Perfect World Paleo Lasagna

Prep Time: 40 minutes
Cook Time: 7 hours
Recipe Makes 10 Servings
Nutritional Breakdown per Serving: 110 calories, 5 grams net carbohydrates, 8 grams fat, 3 grams protein

Ingredients:
¾ pound ground beef
5 minced garlic cloves
1 diced onion
14 ounces diced tomatoes
8 ounces tomato sauce

2 eggplants

3 cups spinach

½ cup pumpkin seeds

1 cup almond milk

2 cups walnuts

1 tsp. nutmeg

½ cup water

1 tbsp. olive oil

Directions:

Begin by slicing your vegetables. It's very important to slice your eggplant long-ways so that you achieve your "noodle" consistency. Next, slice up the onion and the garlic. Place the garlic, onion, and the olive oil in a skillet and cook them until the onions are clear. Add the diced tomatoes to the skillet and cook for an additional minute. Set this aside.

Create your fake cheese sauce by bringing together the pumpkin seeds, walnuts, almond milk, water, and nutmeg. Blend it completely to create a ricotta cheese consistency.

Next, prepare the lasagna in the slow cooker. Pour a layer of tomato sauce on the bottom of the slow cooker and then place down a layer of eggplant noodles. Next, add about half of the spinach to the lasagna. Add half of the fake cheese to the top of the spinach and then add the diced tomato, onion and garlic sauce. Repeat the layering system until you've run out of ingredients. Place the lid on the slow cooker and cook on LOW for seven hours. Enjoy.

Paleo Smashed UP Cauliflower "Potatoes"

Prep Time: 10 minutes
Cook Time: 8 hours
Recipe Makes 8 Servings
Nutritional Breakdown per Serving: 80 calories, 12 grams net carbohydrates per serving, 4 grams fat, 2 grams protein

Ingredients:
1 head of cauliflower
8 minced garlic cloves
1/3 cup chopped dill
1 tbsp. coconut milk
salt and pepper to taste

Directions:
Begin by placing the entire head of cauliflower in the slow cooker—without the leaves and stem. Here in the slow cooker, utilize a small knife to cut the cauliflower into its smaller florets. Toss the garlic and half of the dill into the slow cooker, as well, and add enough water so that some of the cauliflower pieces float. Cook on LOW for eight hours.

Afterwards, drain the slow cooker of the water and remove the remaining mixture. Place the mixture in a large bowl and add the "fresh" dill" and the coconut milk to the cauliflower. Puree the ingredients with a blender or a food processor and enjoy your Paleo mashed potatoes!

CHILIS, SOUPS, AND STEWS

SLOW COOKER

RECIPES

Paleo Perfect Beef Chili

Prep Time: 1 hour
Cook time: 6 hours
Recipe Makes 15 Servings
Nutritional Breakdown Per Serving: 210 calories, 3 grams net carbohydrates, 19 grams fat, 22 grams protein

Ingredients:
4 ½ pounds ground beef
2 diced bell peppers
3 diced onions
4 diced yellow peppers
5 diced jalapeno peppers
3 diced poblano peppers
2 tbsp. oregano leaves
3 tbsp. cumin
3 tbsp. garlic powder
¼ cup beef stock
28 ounces diced tomatoes
2 tbsp. arrowroot powder mixed with 1 tbsp. water
¾ tbsp. cacao powder

Directions:

Begin by browning the beef in a bit of olive oil in a skillet. As it browns for about five minutes, begin chopping your vegetables.

Pour the meat into the slow cooker and follow it with your vegetables. Afterwards, sauté the prepared vegetables in the skillet for a moment—until the onions begin to become clear. Add the tomatoes and stir well prior to pouring the steaming mixture into the slow cooker.

Pour the beef stock into the slow cooker and add all the appropriate spices prior to cooking for 5 hours on LOW. Afterwards, add the arrowroot and water mixture along with the cacao powder and stir well. Cook for an additional hour and serve warm.

Meatball Medley Soup

Prep Time: 10 minutes
Cook Time: 8 hours
Recipe Makes 4 Servings
Nutritional Breakdown per Serving: 275 calories, 5 grams net carbohydrates, 22 grams fat, 23 grams protein

Ingredients:
1 tbsp. olive oil
2 diced onions
3 minced garlic cloves
3 chopped celery stalks
15 ounces crushed tomatoes

1 tsp. oregano

14 ounces beef broth

1 egg

1 pound ground beef

4 tbsp. basil

1/3 cup almond meal

2 tsp. garlic powder

4 cups baby spinach

1 cup broccoli

1 cup cauliflower

1 sliced zucchini

Directions:

Begin by bringing together the celery and the onion in a skillet with the olive oil. Cook them for about ten minutes, until they begin to soften. Afterwards, add the garlic and cook for an additional minute. Pour this mixture into the slow cooker.

Next, pour in the beef broth, remaining vegetables, crushed tomatoes, oregano, basil, and salt into the slow cooker. Place the lid on the slow cooker and allow it to cook for three hours on HIGH.

To the side, as the soup cooks, you must make your meatballs. Stir together the egg, beef, oregano, pepper, and the garlic powder. Stir well and create meatballs. As you create each meatball, plop them into the humming soup. After you've finished allow the soup to cook for an additional hour on HIGH prior to serving. Enjoy.

Red Curry Beef Stew

Prep Time: 20 minutes
Cook Time: 8 hours
Recipe Makes 8 Servings
Nutritional Breakdown per Serving: 250 calories, 7 grams net carbohydrates, 22 grams fat, 23 grams protein

Ingredients:

3 tbsp. coconut oil
2 diced onions
2 ½ pounds beef stew meat
1 can coconut milk
2 tsp. peeled ginger
3 minced garlic cloves
½ cup red curry paste
3 cups chopped broccoli
juice from 1 lime
2 cups diced carrots

Directions:

Begin by placing the coconut oil in the skillet and browning the beef stew meat on all of its sides. Afterwards, transfer these pieces of meat to the slow cooker. Next, sauté the garlic, ginger, and onion in the skillet for an additional five minutes.

Add the coconut milk in order to get all the "scum" off the bottom of the skillet.

Next, add the curry paste, lime juice, the tomato paste, and salt. Stir well, and pour this mixture overtop the meat in the slow cooker. Cook on LOW for eight hours and add the carrots and the broccoli with one hour remaining. Enjoy warm!

Asian Bok Choy Pork Soup

Prep Time: 5 minutes
Cook time: 8 hours.
Recipe Makes 2 Servings.
Nutritional Breakdown Per Serving: 215 calories, 3 grams net carbohydrates, 18 grams fat, 20 grams protein.

Ingredients:
3 cups Bok Choy (alternately, you can use spinach)
4 sliced scallions
1 pound pork
4 minced garlic cloves
4-inch section grated ginger
4 cups chicken stock

Directions:
Begin by pouring the chicken stock into the slow cooker. Toss in the grated ginger and the minced garlic. Next, cube the pork—if you're not using leftovers—and place this in the stock. Add the scallions, as well. Cover this mixture and cook the soup on LOW for eight hours.

When you decide you'd like to eat your soup, place the Bok Choy or spinach into a skillet with a bit of water. When the water begins to boil, add the pork from the slow cooker and sauté it until it's a bit browned. Bring the pork and the Bok Choy into the serving bowls and pour over the rest of the slow cooker broth. Enjoy.

Green Machine Pork Chili

Prep Time: 20 minutes
Cook time: 5 hours
Recipe Makes 8 Servings.
Nutritional Breakdown per Serving: 210 calories, 2 grams net carbohydrates, 20 grams fat, 22 grams protein.

Ingredients:
2 cups chicken stock
1 tsp. cumin
1 tbsp. cilantro
½ cup olive oil
6 minced garlic cloves

1 ½ pounds pork tenderloin

1 pound diced Anaheim chilies

½ tsp. oregano

3 diced jalapenos

1 diced onion

salt and pepper to taste

Directions:

Pour the broth, olive oil, cumin, and oregano into the slow cooker. Stir well. Afterwards, add the rest of the ingredients and set the slow cooker on HIGH. Cook for four hours. After those four hours, shred the pork tenderloin with two forks and allow the slow cooker to cook for an additional hour.

Tropical Coconut Curry Sunny Winter's Day Pork Stew

Prep Time: 15 minutes
Cook Time: 8 hours
Recipe Makes 10 Servings
Nutritional Breakdown per Serving: 275 calories, 5 grams net carbohydrates, 22 grams fat, 25 grams protein

Ingredients:

2 ½ pounds pork tenderloin

3 cups chopped carrots

1 cup pork or chicken broth

1 ½ pounds diced butternut squash

2 tbsp. curry powder

1 tbsp. apple cider vinegar

16 ounces coconut milk

5 minced garlic cloves

salt and pepper to taste

Directions:

Begin by placing the prepared butternut squash and carrots at the very bottom of the slow cooker. Dash with salt and pepper and place the pork tenderloin overtop the vegetables. Salt and pepper the pork, as well. Place the garlic on top of the layers.

Next, pour in the coconut milk, curry powder, and apple cider vinegar. Stir well. Add the broth and continue to stir. Cook the pork on LOW for eight hours. Afterwards, tear apart your pork utilizing two forks. Enjoy warm.

Utterly Kale-Full Chicken Soup

Prep Time: 30 minutes.
Cook Time: 6 hours.
Recipe Makes 6 Servings
Nutritional Breakdown Per Serving: 230 calories, 4 grams net carbohydrates, 12 grams fat, 22 grams protein

Ingredients:
5 cups shredded chicken
5 cups bone broth (or Paleo-friendly broth of your choice)
4 cups kale
4 lemons
1 diced onion
¼ cup olive oil
2 tbsp. lemon juice
Salt and pepper to taste

Directions:
Begin by washing and slicing the kale. Set the kale aside. Next, toss two cups of bone broth, onion, and olive oil into a blender and blend until the mixture is completely assimilated. Pour this creation into the slow cooker.

Next, add the next two cups of bone broth, the shredded chicken, kale, lemon zests, and lemon juice. Salt and pepper the soup, and allow the soup to cook for six hours on LOW. Enjoy.

Puttering Paleo White Chicken Chili

Prep Time: 20 minutes
Cook Time: 6 hours
Recipe Makes 6 Servings
Nutritional Breakdown Per Serving: 210 calories, 2 grams net carbohydrates, 20 grams fat, 22 grams protein

Ingredients:

1 ½ pounds boneless chicken breast

2 diced onions

1 diced green pepper

1 diced onion

5 minced garlic cloves

1 tbsp. cumin

4 cups chicken broth

1 tsp. coriander

4 tbsp. coconut milk

3 tbsp. arrowroot powder

5 ounces green chilies

2 diced jalapenos

Directions:

Begin by slicing and dicing all the vegetables and the chicken. Add everything to the slow cooker and stir well. Place the lid on the slow cooker and cook on LOW for six hours. Shred up the chicken and serve it warm.

Mighty Vegetarian Minestrone Soup

Prep Time: 20 minutes
Cook Time: 8 hours
Recipe Makes 8 Servings
Nutritional Breakdown Per Serving: 210 calories, 13 grams net carbohydrates, 3 grams fat, 5 grams protein

Ingredients:
1 diced sweet potato
2 diced carrots
2 diced zucchini squashes

½ cup spinach

29 ounces diced tomatoes

29 ounces vegetable broth

3 minced garlic cloves

½ tsp. cayenne pepper

1 tsp. oregano

1 tsp. parsley

3 tbsp. olive oil

salt and pepper to taste

Directions:

Begin by pouring the olive oil into the slow cooker and topping it with all the pre-cut vegetables. Pour in the vegetable broth and the tomatoes and stir well. Next, add the spinach and all of the spices. Stir well and cover the slow cooker. Cook on LOW for eight hours. Serve warm.

Better-Netter Butternut Squash Soup

Prep Time: 15 minutes
Cook Time: 8 hours
Recipe Makes 6 Servings
Nutritional Breakdown per Serving: 195 calories, 22 grams net carbohydrates, 9 grams fat, 4 grams protein

Ingredients:

5 cups diced butternut squash
1 diced onion
1 ½ peeled and chopped apples
2 minced garlic cloves
1 ½ tsp. dried thyme
½ tsp. sage
2 cups vegetable stock
1 ½ cup almond milk

Directions:

Bring everything except the almond milk together in a slow cooker and cook the soup on LOW for eight hours. After eight hours, pour in the almond milk and stir well. Pour the soup into a blender and puree the soup until you reach your desired consistency. Salt and pepper to taste, and enjoy.

Creamy Paleo Pumpkin Soup

Prep Time: 10 minutes
Cook time: 6 hours
Recipe Makes 5 Servings
Nutritional Breakdown per Serving: 150 calories, 15 grams net carbohydrates, 12 grams fat, 4 grams protein

Ingredients:

2 diced onions

2 cups vegetable broth

2 minced garlic cloves

4 tbsp. coconut oil

1 can coconut milk

1 tsp. cinnamon

1 tsp. allspice

1 tsp. nutmeg

salt and pepper to taste

Directions:

Begin by heating onions and garlic in coconut oil in a skillet over medium heat. The onions should become clear. Pour this mixture into the slow cooker. Follow the onion mixture with the vegetable broth, coconut milk, cinnamon, allspice, nutmeg, and salt and pepper. Place the lid on the slow cooker and cook on LOW for six hours. Serve warm.

DESSERT
SLOW COOKER
RECIPES

Autumn Arrival Apple Crisp

Prep Time: 15 minutes
Cook Time: 3 hours
Recipe Makes 4 Servings
**Nutritional Breakdown per Serving: 170
calories, 11 grams net carbohydrates, 3
grams fat, 1 gram protein**

Ingredients:
4 Gala apples
¼ cup shredded coconut
1/3 cup almond flour
1/3 cup sliced almonds
3 tbsp. cinnamon

Drizzles of honey

Directions:

Begin by peelings, coring, and chopping up the apples into small pieces. Layer the apples on the bottom of the slow cooker and sprinkle the apples with 1 tbsp. of the cinnamon.

Afterwards, mix together the slivered almonds, almond flour, remaining cinnamon, and the shredded coconut. Sprinkle this onto the apples and drizzle honey over the top. Cook the apples for a full three hours on LOW heat.

Very Berry Crumble

Prep Time: 5 minutes.
Cook Time: 2 hours.
Recipe Makes 5 Servings.
Nutritional Breakdown Per Serving: 280 calories, 10 grams net carbohydrates, 20 grams fat, 4 grams protein.

Ingredients:
4 cups frozen raspberries and blackberries
4 tbsp. melted coconut oil
1 ½ cups almond flour
1 tbsp. honey

Directions:
Begin by placing the various berries in the slow cooker and lending a single tbsp. of the coconut oil to the very center of the berries. To the side, mix together the coconut oil with the almond flour and the honey. Stir well until it begins to seem like almost-wet sand.

Sprinkle this mixture overtop the berries and cook the berry crumble on LOW for two hours.

Impossibly Sweet Potato Brownies

Prep Time: 20 minutes.
Cook Time: 2 hours
Recipe Makes 6 Servings
Nutritional Breakdown per Serving: 210 calories, 7 grams net carbohydrates, 13 grams fat, 4 grams protein

Ingredients:
3 eggs
1 sliced and diced sweet potato
¼ cup honey
¼ cup melted coconut oil
¼ tsp. baking powder
¼ tsp. cinnamon
2 tbsp. cocoa powder
4 tbsp. coconut flour
½ tsp. vanilla extract

Directions:
Begin by prepping the sweet potato by stabbing it a few times and placing it in your microwave for about fifteen minutes. Afterwards, peel it and mash it up. Stir in the rest of the ingredients: whisked eggs, melted coconut oil, vanilla, and

honey. Stir well. Add the rest of the ingredients: cocoa powder, coconut flour, baking powder, salt, and cinnamon. Stir well.

Formulate each brownie into a ball—about one inch by one inch, and place each ball in the slow cooker. Place the lid on the slow cooker and allow the sweet potato brownie balls to cook for a full two hours on LOW.

Fall-Into-Pumpkin Pudding

Prep Time: 5 minutes
Cook Time: 7 hours
Recipe Makes 8 Servings
Nutritional Breakdown per Serving: 210 calories, 18 grams net carbohydrates, 23 grams fat, 8 grams protein

Ingredients:

4 tbsp. melted coconut oil

2 cups coconut milk

4 cups pumpkin puree

3 eggs

½ cup maple syrup

4 tbsp. coconut flour

1 ½ tbsp. vanilla extract

1 tsp. baking powder

Directions:

Bring all the ingredients into the slow cooker and stir well. Plop the top on the slow cooker and allow the pudding to cook for a full seven hours on LOW. The pudding will appear to have a crust, but it will be perfect beneath.

Sweet Carolina Slow Cooker Applesauce

Prep Time: 15 minutes
Cook Time: 3 hours
Recipe Makes 12 Servings
Nutritional Breakdown Per Serving: 120 calories, 18 grams net carbohydrates, 12 grams fat, 3 grams protein

Ingredients:
12 honey crisp or granny smith apples
3 tbsp. melted coconut oil
2 tsp. cinnamon
¼ tsp. salt
juice from 1 lemon

Directions:
Begin by placing the pre-melted coconut oil into the slow cooker. Spread this oil all over the slow cooker. Next, core, peel and slice up the apples. Layer the apples in the bottom of the slow cooker and then squeeze out the lemon onto them. Sprinkle over the cinnamon and the salt and stir well.

Cover the slow cooker and heat the apples on HIGH for two hours. Afterwards, stir and turn the slow cooker to low. Allow the apples to cook for an additional hour. Stir to achieve your desired applesauce consistency.

Conclusion

"Paleo Slow Cooker Cookbook" takes you on a journey to better nutritive understanding. Armed with the forty recipes, you can truly take hold of your life and your schedule once more. You can toss a few funny-looking naked ingredients into a slow cooker in the morning and come home to a full-blown feast in the evening. While you're out living your crazy life, your body will be reaping the rewards of the essential nutrients brought in by your new Paleo lifestyle. You'll lose weight, build muscle, relieve anxiety, and find greater reason to fuel yourself well. Find reasons to utilize the slow cooker this fall and this winter. Your soul—and your waistline—will thank you.